"Now, I feel confident and optimistic about my upcoming English exam and about grammar in general."

- Zack, High School Student

"The way that Elizabeth teaches is so impressive. I have no words to describe it. It really inspired me and my kids."

- Drinayat, Teacher

"I am studying for the GMAT and have found your website and diagramming books to be invaluable!"

- Karen-Kim, Student

"I will begin teaching 8th grade English in a few months, and your website and products are going to give me so much more confidence and structure! I am so glad I found you!"

- Katherine, Teacher

"I feel more equipped to explore a whole new world of knowledge simply because I am armed with a fuller understanding of how the sentence works."

- Phil, Writer

"Your materials are a life-saver and a confidence-booster!"

- Lori, Grammar Lover

"Your materials helped me break down complex ideas and present them in simple, easy-to-understand ways.

My kids did great! Week after week, they had a blast parsing, diagramming, and composing sentences galore. No joke. They loved it!

One student did so well on my final exam that his test grade was 104%!

Your materials were invaluable."

- Teresa, Homeschool Teacher

"I operate a small school in Thailand. I recently bought your book and have been using it to teach my students and myself. My students and I love it."

- Charles, Teacher & Principal

© www.English-Grammar-Revolution.com

STAY SMART

WORKBOOK

188 ADVANCED SENTENCE DIAGRAMMING EXERCISES

BY ELIZABETH O'BRIEN

EDITED BY DAVID O'BRIEN

www.English-Grammar-Revolution.com

ISBN-13: 978-1470051105
ISBN-10: 1470051109

CONTENTS

INTRODUCTION

Did you know that many students today aren't taught grammar?

It's true. That was my experience through high school, and it lead me to feel self-conscious about my writing and speaking for a very long time.

Things changed for me when I entered one of my English classes in college. I was lucky enough to have a fabulous professor who taught me grammar and sentence diagramming. Finally, everything made sense, and it felt great!

I assume that since you have this book in front of you, you were also lucky enough to have a fabulous teacher teach the same things to you.

You know how important grammar is to a person's thought process, and you've seen the positive effects that grammar and diagramming have had on your writing and your confidence.

As with most things in life, it's easy to forget what we've learned if we're not putting it into practice every day. That's why this book of sentence diagramming exercises is sitting in front of you.

The material in this book will enable you to remember and review all of the information you've already learned.

This book will help you continue to be a knowledgeable student who's ready to take on the world!

Enjoy these sentence diagrams.

Happy Learning,

Elizabeth

Elizabeth O'Brien

www.English-Grammar-Revolution.com

HOW TO USE THIS BOOK

The Right Tools

It's important to have the right tools for any job.

I suggest diagramming these sentences with a **ruler** and a **pencil** that has a good eraser.

The pencil and eraser will allow you to easily make changes to your diagrams, and the ruler will help you make your diagrams neat and precise.

They'll look like little pieces of art when you're done!

Where To Start

I suggest starting with the review material that begins on the next page.

Reviewing is a good idea for a couple of reasons.

1. It will help you remember what you've learned.

2. It will familiarize you with this book.

After reviewing, you'll be ready to start diagramming.

Have fun!

THE 8 PARTS OF SPEECH

Every single word belongs to one of eight word groups. We call these groups the **parts of speech**.

Here, you'll find a brief definition, a few examples, and a few sentence diagrams for each part of speech.

1. Nouns name people, places, things, or ideas.

Examples: book, matches, sunlight, Maria, baby, shell

I saw the <u>movie</u> in the <u>theater</u>.

The <u>fish</u> swam through the <u>water</u> in the <u>pond</u>.

2. Pronouns take the place of one or more nouns.

Examples: I, you, me, they, who, which, yourself

Would <u>you</u> like to go with <u>me</u> to the beach?

Betty, stop looking at <u>yourself</u> in the mirror.

Diagramming Nouns & Pronouns

Nouns and pronouns can perform many jobs in sentences.

They can act as subjects, direct objects, indirect objects, objects of prepositions, predicate nouns, and more!

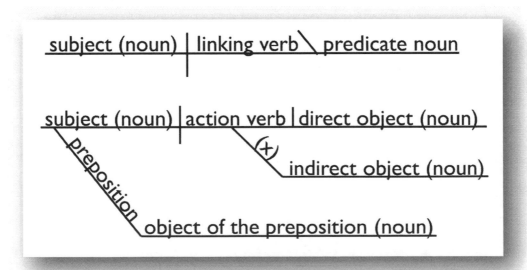

3. Verbs show action or a state of being.

Examples: eat, find, run, walk, become, feel, seem, are

The baker <u>cut</u> the bread. (action verb)

The bread <u>is</u> good. (linking verb)

Diagramming Verbs

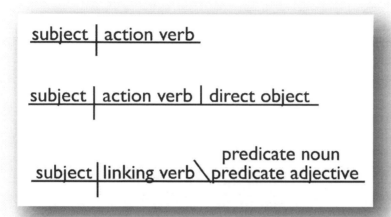

See *The Verb Chart* on page 12 for more information.

4. Adjectives describe nouns and pronouns.

They tell us: **Which one? What kind? How many? Whose?**

Examples: the, orange, special, many, colorful, Charlie's

I would like <u>the</u> <u>fresh</u> muffin.

<u>The</u> <u>blue</u> coat is <u>mine</u>.

Diagramming Adjectives

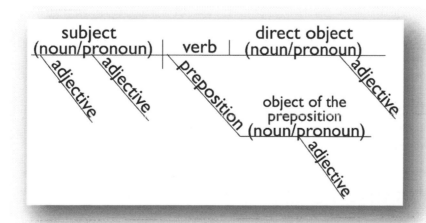

5. Adverbs describe verbs, adjectives, and other adverbs.

They tell us: **How? When? Where? Why? To what extent?**

Examples: awkwardly, lazily, silently, stylishly, well, yesterday, very, so

My friend dresses <u>so</u> <u>stylishly.</u>

<u>Yesterday,</u> we went shopping <u>everywhere</u>!

Diagramming Adverbs

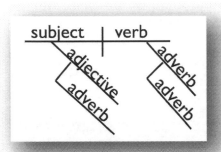

6. Prepositions show the relationship between a noun or a pronoun (called the *object of the preposition*) and some other word or element in the rest of the sentence.

Prepositions are always in prepositional phrases (a **preposition** + a <u>noun</u> or <u>pronoun</u> + any modifiers of the noun or pronoun). Prepositional phrases act as adjectives or adverbs.

Examples: above, behind, below, from, inside, up, over

*Will you walk **with** <u>me</u>?*

*The monkey **with** <u>stripes</u> is cute.*

Diagramming Prepositions

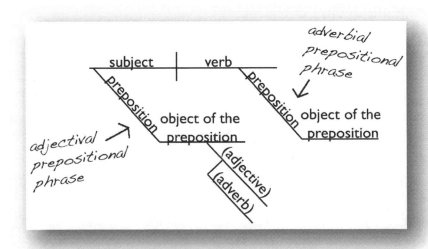

7. Conjunctions join two or more words, phrases, or clauses.

Coordinating conjunctions (*for, and, nor, but or, yet, so*) join equals.

> *Can we go to the zoo <u>and</u> the fair?*

Subordinating conjunctions (*whenever, because, although, since, if, before...*) join independent clauses with dependent clauses.

> *<u>Although</u> that would be nice, we can only go to the zoo.*

Diagramming Coordinating & Subordinating Conjunction

The way to diagram conjunctions depends greatly on the sentence. This is just one example.

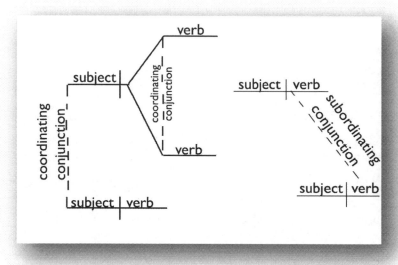

8. Interjections show emotion. They are not grammatically related to the rest of the sentence.

> Examples: rats, gee, darn, oh no, aw, gosh, yes, fiddlesticks, holy cow

> *<u>Oh no</u>, we lost the game.*

> *<u>Holy cow</u>! This cake is delicious!*

Diagramming Interjections

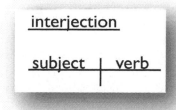

THE VERB CHART

There are four types of main verbs.

⇓ TRANSITIVE VERBS ⇓ (Carry an action to a receiver)	⇓ INTRANSITIVE VERBS ⇓ (Do not carry an action to a receiver)
1. Transitive Active Action verb Subject performs the action Direct object receives the action *I ate the cake.* *Joe kicked the ball.* subject | verb | direct object	**2. Intransitive Complete** Action verb Subject performs the action NO receiver of the action *My sister smiled.* *The boy ran.* subject | verb
3. Transitive Passive Action verb, always in verb phrase Subject receives action Doer of action may be shown in a prepositional phrase *The vase was broken by Kevin.* *My car was stolen.* subject | verb	**4. Intransitive Linking** NOT an action verb - a verb of BEING Verb acts like an equals sign Links the subject with a predicate noun or a predicate adjective *Mr. Black became a teacher.* *George was happy.* predicate noun/ subject | linking verb \ predicate adjective

List of Linking Verbs: be, am, is, are, was, were, been, being, become, seem, appear, look, feel, sound, taste, smell, remain, grow, stay, turn

List of Helping Verbs: be, am, is, are, was, were, been, being, have, has, had, could, should, would, may, might, must, shall, can, will, do, did, does, having

Helping verbs are not main verbs. They are used in verb phrases.

© www.English-Grammar-Revolution.com

PHRASES

Phrases are groups of words without both a subject and a verb. They function as a single part of speech.

Phrases are made up of multiple words which each have their own function, but all of the words work together to perform one larger function.

There are many types of phrases.

1. **Verb phrases** are made of one or more helping verb and one main verb.

   Verb phrases function as verbs.

   I could have eaten six cookies!   *Have you been sitting in my chair?*

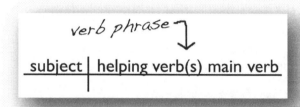

2. **Prepositional phrases** must have a preposition and an object of the preposition (noun or pronoun). They may also contain adjectives and adverbs.

   Prepositional phrases function as adjectives or adverbs.

   We walked around town. I like coffee with cream.

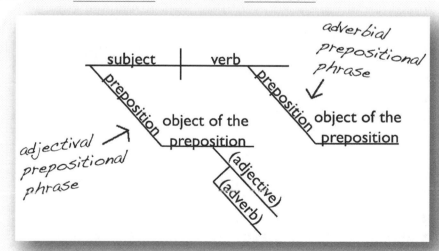

Note: For information on gerund, infinitive, and participial phrases, see *Verbals* on pages 19 - 22.

CLAUSES

A clause is a group of words with a subject and a verb.

There are two main types of clauses.

1. Independent clauses express complete thoughts.

Birds sing.   *My favorite red birds sing beautiful songs.*

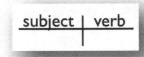

2. Dependent clauses (also called *subordinate clauses*) do not express complete thoughts. They need to be joined to independent clauses in order to make sense.

Dependent clauses are similar to phrases because all of the words in a dependent clause come together to function as one part of speech.

There are three basic types of dependent clauses: noun clauses, adjective clauses, and adverb clauses.

> **a. Noun clauses** are dependent clauses that act as nouns.
>
> They can perform any of the noun jobs (subject, direct object, indirect object, object of the preposition, predicate noun...).
>
> Here is a diagram of a noun clause acting as the subject of the independent clause.

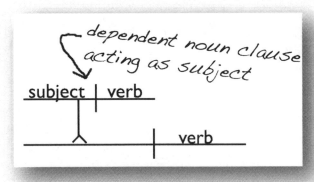

> Noun clauses may be introduced by the following words:
>
> *that, if, whether, who, whom, whose, which, what, when, where, how why, whoever, whenever, whatever, wherever, however, whichever, whomever*
>
> Some people call these words *noun clause markers*. They are words that tell us that a noun clause is coming.

Whatever you want is fine with me.

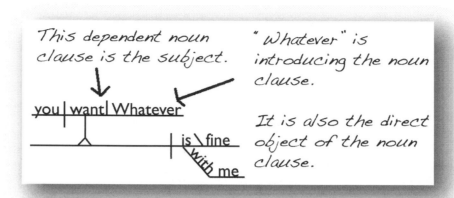

Whatever is introducing this noun clause, and it is the direct object of the noun clause. The whole noun clause is acting as the subject of the independent clause.

Notice that *whatever* also has its own job in the sentence. It is the direct object of the noun clause.

Sometimes, the word introducing the noun clause doesn't have any other function in the sentence except to introduce it.

When the word introducing a noun clause has no other function in the clause except to introduce it, the word is called an *expletive*.

We diagram expletives on **skyhooks**, which are lines that float above the noun clause.

My mother knows that I love the library.

Notice that *that* isn't performing any other job in the noun clause.

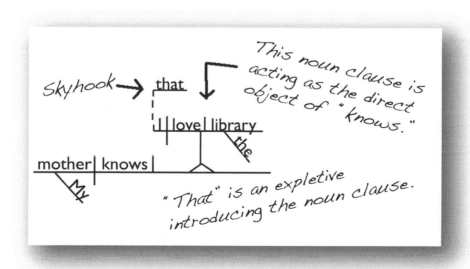

Sometimes, noun clauses don't have a word introducing them.

My mother knows <u>I love the library</u>.

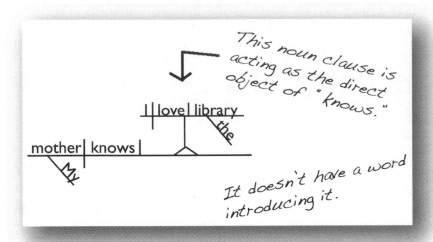

This noun clause acting as the direct object does not have a word introducing it. That's okay!

b. Adjective clauses are dependent clauses that act as adjectives.

Adjective clauses often begin with relative pronouns (who, whom, whose, that, which) or relative adverbs (where, when, why).

Sometimes, adjective clauses don't have a word introducing them.

Here's an example of an adjective clause modifying the subject of the independent clause.

The relative pronoun is also acting as the subject of the adjective clause:

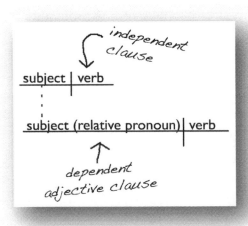

Adjective Clause With Relative Pronoun

The woman <u>who looked happy</u> danced.

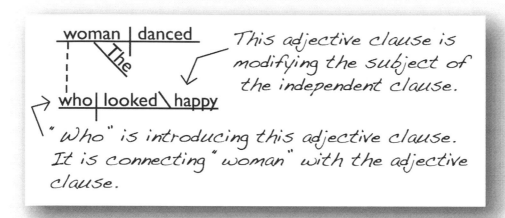

Who is a relative pronoun introducing the adjective clause and acting as the subject of the adjective clause.

This is an adjective clause because the whole clause is modifying the noun *woman*.

Adjective Clause With Relative Adverb

This is the park <u>where we played</u>.

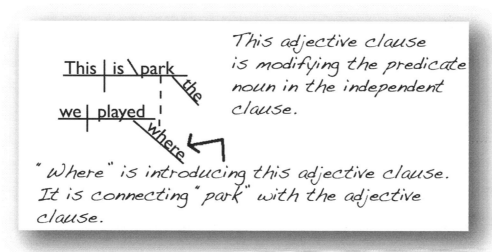

Where is a relative adverb introducing the adjective clause. The clause is an adjective clause because it's modifying the noun *park*.

Where is also acting as an adverb in the dependent adjective clause.

c. Adverb clauses are dependent clauses that act as adverbs.

They are introduced by subordinating conjunctions (because, when, if, whenever, until...).

Diagram the subordinating conjunction on a slated, dotted line between the independent clause and the adverb clause.

I read <u>because I love stories</u>.   *My dad smiled <u>when I made dinner</u>.*

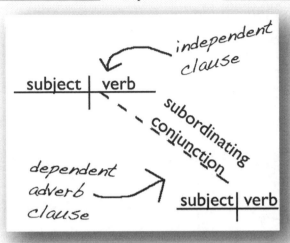

Elliptical clauses are a type of dependent clause that have some of the words implied. Diagram the implied words in parentheses.

David is faster <u>than his brother (is fast)</u>.

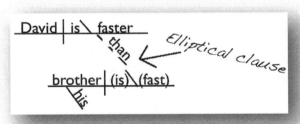

I like coffee <u>more than (I like) tea.</u>

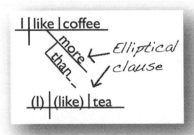

VERBALS

Verbals are formed from verbs but don't act as verbs. They act as nouns, adverbs, or adjectives.

There are three kinds of verbals: infinitives, participles, and gerunds.

1. Infinitives are formed from the word *to* and a verb. These two words act together as nouns, adverbs, or adjectives.

I love <u>to laugh</u>. (direct object - noun)

The person <u>to call</u> is Joan. (adjective)

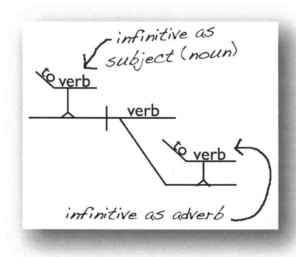

Bare Infinitives

Sometimes, infinitives are missing the word *to*. This often happens after verbs like *see, let, watch,* and *make.*

I let her <u>play</u> outside.

These are called *bare infinitives.* Diagram them as you normally would, but put the word *to* in parentheses.

Infinitive Phrases

Infinitives are formed from verbs, and they act as nouns, adjectives, or adverbs. Since they are formed from verbs, they maintain some of their "verb-ness" even though they don't function as verbs.

They can have direct objects, predicate nouns, predicate adjectives, "subjects," adjectives and adverbs. The "subject" of an infinitive will be in the objective case (me, him, her).

When an infinitive has any of these complements or modifiers, the words work together to form an infinitive phrase. The whole phrase performs the job of a noun, adjective, or adverb.

- *I love to laugh loudly at the movies.*

  infinitive + adverb + prepositional phrase = infinitive phrase, noun - direct object of the verb *love*

- *The person to call for help is Joan.*

  infinitive + prepositional phrase = infinitive phrase, adjective modifying *person*

- *I want her to call the pizza place.*

  "subject" + infinitive + adjectives + direct object = infinitive phrase, noun - direct object of the verb *want*

Diagramming Infinitive Phrases

This diagram shows some possible forms of an infinitive phrase. There is a lot of variation both in how infinitive phrases act and what words they can contain.

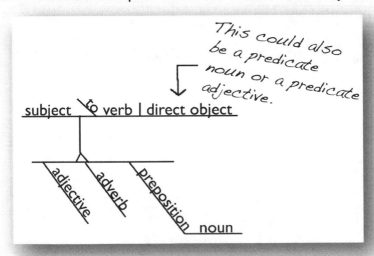

Put the little tree in the space within the sentence diagram that corresponds with how the infinitive phrase is acting (noun, adjective, or adverb).

© www.English-Grammar-Revolution.com

2. Participles are formed from a verb + *-ing, -d, -t, -n.* They act as adjectives.

Shooting stars are beautiful. (adjective)

This is burned toast! (adjective)

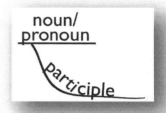

Let's have frozen food. (adjective)

Participial Phrases

Since participles are formed from verbs, they maintain some of their "verb-ness." They can have direct objects, predicate nouns, or predicate adjectives. They can be modified by adverbs or adjectives.

When a participle has any of these complements or modifiers, the words work together to form a participial phrase. The whole phrase performs the job of an adjective.

- *Stars shooting across the sky are beautiful.*

  participle + prepositional phrase = participial phrase, adjective

- *This terribly burned toast actually tastes amazing.*

  adverb + participle = participial phrase, adjective

- *Kicking the ball across the field, he won the game.*

  participle + direct object + prepositional phrase = participial phrase, adjective

Diagramming Participial Phrases

Diagram the participle on a slanted, curved line below the noun or pronoun that it modifies. Diagram the participle's complements and modifiers as shown.

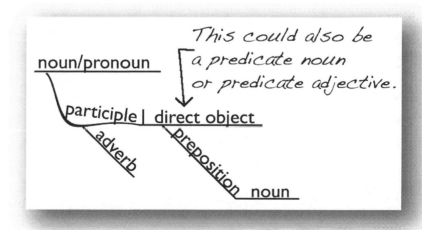

3. Gerunds are formed from a verb + *-ing*. They act as nouns, and they can perform any of the noun jobs (subject, direct object, indirect object, object of the preposition...)

Running is fun.
(subject, noun)

I love *diagramming*.
(direct object, noun)

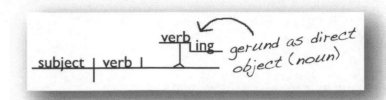

I received an award for *running*. (object of the preposition, noun)

Gerund Phrases

Since gerunds are formed from verbs, they maintain some of their "verb-ness" even though they act as nouns. They can have direct objects, predicate nouns, predicate adjectives, or "subjects." They can also be modified by adverbs or adjectives. The "subject" of a gerund is always in the possessive case (his, hers, Jim's).

When a gerund has any of these complements or modifiers, the words work together to form a gerund phrase. The whole phrase performs the job of a noun.

* *Running around the lake* is fun.

    gerund + prepositional phrase = gerund phrase, subject - noun

* I love *diagramming sentences*.

    gerund + direct object = gerund phrase, direct object - noun

* *Jim's snoring* is keeping me awake.

    "subject" + gerund = gerund phrase, subject - noun

Diagramming Gerund Phrases

Diagram the gerund on a step with the *-ing* on the bottom part of the step. Attach the complements and modifiers as shown.

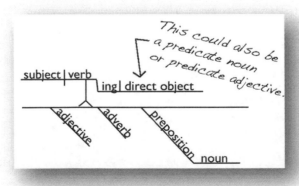

© www.English-Grammar-Revolution.com

TACKLING SENTENCES: DIAGRAMMING TIPS

Some sentences are long and complicated, and the task of diagramming them can be overwhelming. Sometimes, it can be difficult to know where to start.

I'll share my thought process with you as we diagram a sentence together. Feel free to use my process or your own!

Whenever my alarm beeps, I jump out of bed.

Step 1: Identify the independent clause(s).

I jump out of bed (independent clause)

Step 2: Identify and diagram each part of the independent clause(s). This includes subjects, verbs, complements, modifiers, and anything else in the clause!

I = subject (pronoun)

jump = verb (intransitive complete)

out of bed = prepositional phrase (adverb)

out of = preposition (both words are working together)

bed = object of the preposition (noun)

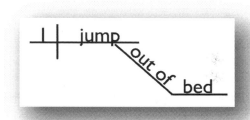

Step 3: If the sentence has any dependent clauses, figure out what they are modifying.

Whenever my alarm beeps (dependent adverb clause modifying "jump")

Step 4: Identify and diagram each part of the dependent clause.

Whenever = subordinating conjunction

alarm = subject (of dependent clause)

my = adjective

beeps = verb (of dependent clause) (intransitive complete)

Yay! It's time to start diagramming!

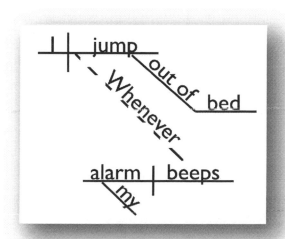

SENTENCE # 1

Cheetahs can change direction in midair when they chase prey.

Every sentence in this book has a chart like the one below. Some of the spaces in each chart are blank.

Fill in the blanks with the correct word(s). I've filled in this chart as an example for you.

Key	
Cheetahs can change direction in midair	independent clause
cheetahs	subject (of independent clause) (noun)
can change	verb phrase
can	helping verb
change	main verb (transitive active)
direction	direct object (noun)
in midair	prepositional phrase (adverb)
in	preposition
midair	object of the preposition (noun)
when they chase prey	dependent clause (adverb)
when	subordinating conjunction
they	subject (of dependent clause) (pronoun)
chase	verb (transitive active)
prey	direct object (noun)

SENTENCE # 2

A sheep, a duck, and a rooster were the first passengers on a hot-air balloon.

Key	
A sheep, a duck, and a rooster were the first passengers on a hot-air balloon.	independent clause
	compound subjects (nouns)
a, a, a	adjectives
	coordinating conjunction
	main verb (intransitive linking)
passengers	predicate noun
the, first	
on a hot air balloon	prepositional phrase (adjective)
on	
balloon	
a, hot-air	adjectives

SENTENCE # 3

A bat can eat 3,000 insects in one night.

Key	
A bat can eat 3,000 insects in one night.	independent clause
	subject (noun)
A	adjective
	verb phrase
	helping verb
	main verb (transitive active)
insects	direct object (noun)
3,000	adjective
	prepositional phrase (adverb)
in	
night	
one	adjective

SENTENCE # 4

The creators of Star Wars designed Yoda to look like Albert Einstein.

Tip: *To look like Albert Einstein* is your first <u>infinitive phrase</u> in this book! Remember that infinitives and infinitive phrases can act as nouns, adjectives, or adverbs.

Key	
The creators of Star Wars designed Yoda to look like Albert Einstein.	independent clause
	subject (noun)
The	
	prepositional phrase (adjective)
of	
Star Wars	object of the preposition (proper noun)
designed	verb (transitive active)
Yoda	direct object (proper noun)
to look like Albert Einstein	
to look	infinitive
like Albert Einstein	prepositional phrase (adverb)
like	
	object of the preposition (proper noun)

SENTENCE # 5

In Japan, you can buy watermelons that are shaped like pyramids.

Key	
In Japan, you can buy watermelons	independent clause
	subject (of independent clause) (pronoun)
can buy	
can	
buy	
	direct object (noun)
In Japan	prepositional phrase (adverb)
In	
	object of the preposition (proper noun)
that are shaped like pyramids	dependent clause (adjective, modifying "watermelons")
	subject (of dependent clause) (relative pronoun introducing adjective clause)
are	
shaped	predicate adjective
like pyramids	prepositional phrase (adverb)
	preposition
pyramids	

SENTENCE # 6

Early American settlers made gum from spruce sap and beeswax.

Key	
Early American settlers made gum from spruce sap and beeswax.	independent clause
settlers	
American	proper adjective
Early	
made	
gum	
from spruce sap and beeswax	prepositional phrase (adverb)
from	
	compound objects of the preposition (nouns)
spruce	adjective
and	

SENTENCE # 7

A man knotted 39 cherry stems with his tongue in three minutes.

Key	
A man knotted 39 cherry stems with his tongue in three minutes.	independent clause
	subject (noun)
	adjective
	verb (transitive active)
	direct object (noun)
in three minutes	prepositional phrase (adverb)
in	
minutes	
three	
with his tongue	
with	
tongue	
his	
39	
cherry	

SENTENCE # 8

In Siberia, solid blocks of tea were used as money until the 19th century.

Key	
In Siberia, solid blocks of tea were used as money until the nineteenth century.	independent clause
blocks	
were used	
	helping verb
	main verb (intransitive complete)
solid	adjective
of tea	
of	
tea	
In Siberia	
In	
Siberia	
until the 19th century	prepositional phrase (adverb)
until	
century	
the, 19th	adjectives
as money	prepositional phrase (adverb)
as	
money	

SENTENCE # 9

Some cockroaches can survive without air for 45 minutes.

Key	
Some cockroaches can survive without air for 45 minutes.	independent clause
cockroaches	
Some	
can survive	verb phrase
	helping verb
	main verb (intransitive complete)
without air	
without	
air	
for 45 minutes	
for	
minutes	object of the preposition (noun)
45	adjective

SENTENCE # 10

Nouns are words that name people, places, things, or ideas.

Key	
Nouns are words	independent clause
Nouns	subject (of independent clause)(noun)
are	
words	
that name people, places, things, or ideas	dependent clause (adjective – modifying "words")
	subject (of dependent clause) (relative pronoun introducing adjective clause)
name	verb (transitive active)
people, places, things, ideas	
or	

SENTENCE # 11

A violin contains 70 pieces of wood.

Key	
A violin contains 70 pieces of wood.	independent clause
	subject (noun)
A	
	verb (transitive active)
	direct object (noun)
70	
of wood	
of	
	object of the preposition (noun)

SENTENCE # 12

The first product with a barcode was Wrigley's gum.

Key	
The first product with a barcode was Wrigley's gum.	independent clause
	subject (noun)
The, first	
with a barcode	
with	
barcode	
	verb (intransitive linking)
gum	
Wrigley's	

SENTENCE # 13

Ancient Egyptians slept on stone pillows.

Key	
Ancient Egyptians slept on stone pillows.	independent clause
	subject (proper noun)
Ancient	
slept	
	prepositional phrase (adverb)
	preposition
	object of the preposition (noun)
	adjective

SENTENCE # 14

In one year, the average American drinks over 300 sodas.

Tip: Up until now, all of the numbers in these sentences have been acting as adjectives, but *300* is acting as a noun.

Key	
In one year, the average American drinks over 300 sodas.	independent clause
	subject (proper noun)
	verb (transitive active)
	direct object (noun)
the, average	
In one year	
In	
year	
one	
over 300	
over	
300	

SENTENCE # 15

New York's Empire State building was built with ten million bricks.

Tip: Treat *ten million* as one word.

Key	
New York's Empire State building was built with ten million bricks.	independent clause
Empire State Building	
	verb phrase
	helping verb
	verb (intransitive complete)
New York's	
with ten million bricks	
with	
bricks	
ten million	adjective

SENTENCE # 16

Jellyfish can sting when they are alive or dead.

Key	
Jellyfish can sting	independent clause
	subject (of independent clause) (noun)
can sting	
can	
sting	
when they are alive or dead	dependent clause (adverb)
	subordinating conjunction
	subject (of dependent clause) (pronoun)
	verb (intransitive linking)
alive, dead	compound predicate adjectives
	coordinating conjunction

SENTENCE # 17

Giraffes can clean their ears with their long tongues.

Key	
Giraffes can clean their ears with their long tongues.	independent clause
Giraffes	
can clean	
can	
clean	
ears	
their	
with their long tongues	
with	
tongues	
	adjectives

SENTENCE # 18

An adjective is a word that describes a noun or a pronoun.

Key	
An adjective is a word	independent clause
adjective	
An	
	verb (intransitive linking)
	predicate noun
that describes a noun or a pronoun	dependent clause (adjective)
	subject (of dependent clause) (relative pronoun introducing adjective clause)
describes	
noun, pronoun	
a, a	
or	

SENTENCE # 19

Bolts of lightning can shoot out of erupting volcanoes.

Tips: Some prepositions like *out of* are made from more than one word. Treat these two words as one preposition.

Erupting is your first participle in this book! Yay!

Key	
Bolts of lightning can shoot out of erupting volcanoes.	independent clause
Bolts	
can shoot	
	helping verb
	main verb (intransitive complete)
of lightning	
of	
lightning	
out of erupting volcanoes	
out of	preposition
	object of the preposition (noun)
	participle (adjective)

© www.English-Grammar-Revolution.com

SENTENCE # 20

Crayola makes 29 shades of red crayons.

Key	
Crayola makes 29 shades of red crayons.	independent clause
	subject (proper noun)
makes	
	direct object (noun)
29	
	prepositional phrase (adjective)
	preposition
	object of the preposition (noun)
	adjective

SENTENCE # 21

When cats are happy, they close their eyes tightly.

Key	
they close their eyes tightly	independent clause
	subject (of independent clause) (pronoun)
	verb (transitive active)
	direct object (noun)
	adjective
	adverb
When cats are happy	dependent clause (adverb)
	subordinating conjunction
	subject (of dependent clause) (noun)
	verb (intransitive linking)
	predicate adjective

© www.English-Grammar-Revolution.com

SENTENCE # 22

Napoleon Hill said, "The starting point of all achievement is desire."

Tips: *The starting point of all achievement is desire* is a dependent noun clause acting as the direct object of the verb *said.*

This sentence has a participle modifying the subject of the noun clause.

Key	
Napoleon Hill said, ("The starting point of all achievement is desire.")	independent clause
Napoleon Hill	
said	
The starting point of all achievement is desire	dependent clause (direct object) (noun)
point	subject (of dependent clause) (noun)
The	
starting	participle (adjective)
of all achievement	
of	
achievement	
all	
is	verb (of dependent clause) (intransitive linking)
desire	predicate noun

SENTENCE # 23

Marty's mother, the town's librarian*, is beautiful and kind.

Librarian is an appositive. Appositives are nouns that rename other nouns.

This appositive renames the subject. Diagram it in parenthesis on the same line as the subject.

Key	
Marty's mother, the town's librarian, is beautiful and kind.	independent clause
	subject (noun)
	appositive (noun renaming the subject)
Marty's	
the, town's	
is	
	compound predicate adjectives
	coordinating conjunction

SENTENCE # 24

Pumice is the only rock that floats in water.

Key	
Pumice is the only rock	independent clause
Pumice	
is	
rock	
the, only	
that floats in water	dependent clause (adjective)
that	subject (of dependent clause) (relative pronoun introducing adjective clause)
floats	
in water	
in	
water	

SENTENCE # 25

You can't hum if you plug your nose.

Key	
You can't hum	independent clause
	subject (of independent clause) (pronoun)
	verb phrase
	helping verb
	main verb (intransitive complete)
n't (not)	adverb (Negatives like "not" and "never" are adverbs.)
if you plug your nose	
if	
you	
plug	
nose	
your	

SENTENCE # 26

You can see autumn leaves from space.

Key	
You can see autumn leaves from space.	independent clause
You	
can see	
	helping verb
	main verb (transitive active)
	direct object (noun)
	adjective
	prepositional phrase (adverb)
	preposition
	object of the preposition (noun)

SENTENCE # 27

Diagram the following Christopher Columbus quote.

"You can never cross the ocean unless you have the courage to lose sight of the shore."

Tip: *To lose sight of the shore* is an infinitive phrase.

Key	
You can never cross the ocean	independent clause
You	
can cross	
can	
cross	
never	
ocean	
	adjective

© www.English-Grammar-Revolution.com

unless you have the courage to lose sight of the shore	
	subordinating conjunction
	subject (of dependent clause) (pronoun)
	verb (transitive active)
	direct object (noun)
the	
to lose sight of the shore	adjective (infinitive phrase modifying "courage")
to lose	
	direct object of infinitive (noun)
of the shore	prepositional phrase (adjective)
of	
shore	
the	

SENTENCE # 28

Diagram this Hans Christian Andersen quote. It's two sentences, so you'll have to make two sentence diagrams.

"Just living is not enough. One must have sunshine, freedom, and a little flower."

Tip: *Just living* is your first gerund phrase in this book! Gerund phrases act as nouns.

Key	
Just living is not enough.	independent clause
living	subject (gerund - noun)
Just	adverb (modifying "living" – Gerunds act as nouns but can take adverbial modifiers.)
is	

© www.English-Grammar-Revolution.com

	predicate adjective
not	
One must have sunshine, freedom, and a little flower.	independent clause
One	
must have	
must	
have	
	compound direct objects
	coordinating conjunction
a, little	

SENTENCE # 29

A dolphin can learn to recognize itself in the mirror.

Tip: This sentence contains an infinitive phrase.

Key	
A dolphin can learn to recognize itself in the mirror.	independent clause
dolphin	
A	
can learn	
can	
learn	
to recognize itself in the mirror	
to recognize	infinitive
itself	direct object of infinitive (pronoun)
in the mirror	
in	
mirror	
the	

SENTENCE # 30

Chicks can breathe through their shells.

Key	
Chicks can breathe through their shells.	independent clause
	subject (noun)
	verb phrase
	helping verb
	main verb (intransitive complete)
	prepositional phrase (adverb)
	preposition
	object of the preposition (noun)
	adjective

SENTENCE # 31

Whenever she sees a movie, my sister says that she'll be a movie star someday.

Tip: The direct object of the independent clause is the dependent noun clause *that she'll be a movie star someday*. *That* is introducing the noun clause. It has no other function in the clause except to introduce it. Because of this, it's called an expletive, and it sits on a "skyhook." Read more on page 15.

Fun Fact: Did you notice that *movie* is used as two different parts of speech in this sentence?

Key	
my sister says (that she'll be a movie star someday)	independent clause
sister	subject (of independent clause) (noun)
my	
says	

	dependent clause (direct object) (noun)
	word introducing noun clause (expletive) (sits on a *skyhook*)
she	subject (of dependent noun clause) (pronoun)
'll be (will be)	verb phrase
'll (will)	
be	
	predicate noun
a, movie	
someday	
	dependent clause (adverb)
Whenever	
	subject (of dependent clause) (pronoun)
	verb (transitive active)
	direct object (noun)
a	

SENTENCE # 32

In the open ocean, tsunamis sometimes travel as fast as jets.

Tip: This sentence has an **elliptical clause**, a type of dependent clause that has some implied words. Diagram the implied words in parentheses.

It's as if this says ...*as fast as jets (travel).*

Fast is an adverb modifying *travel*. The first *as* is an adverb modifying *fast*, and the second *as* is a subordinating conjunction introducing the elliptical clause.

This may be the first time you've diagrammed an elliptical clause. Use what you know and give it a try! (Page 18 has information on elliptical clauses.)

Key	
In the open ocean, tsunamis sometimes travel as fast	independent clause
tsunamis	
travel	
sometimes	
In the open ocean	
In	

ocean	
the, open	
fast	adverb (modifying "travel")
as	adverb (modifying "fast")
as jets (travel)	dependent clause (adverb- elliptical clause)
as	subordinating conjunction (modifying "as")
jets	subject (of elliptical clause) (noun)
(travel)	implied verb of elliptical clause (intransitive complete)

SENTENCE # 33

Owls can't move their eyeballs.

Key	
Owls can't move their eyeballs.	independent clause
Owls	
can move	
can	
move	
't (not)	
eyeballs	
their	

SENTENCE # 34

Mark kicked the ball as hard as Nate did.

Tip: Look! *As hard as Nate did (kick the ball)* is another elliptical clause!

Key	
Mark kicked the ball as hard	independent clause
Mark	
kicked	
ball	
the	
hard	adverb (modifying "kicked")
as	adverb (modifying "hard")
as Nate did (kick the ball)	dependent clause (adverb- elliptical clause)
as	subordinating conjunction modifying "as"
	subject (of elliptical clause) (proper noun)
did (kick)	
did	
(kick)	implied main verb of elliptical clause (transitive active)
(ball)	implied direct object of elliptical clause (noun)
(the)	implied adjective

SENTENCE # 35

Rolling onto his stomach, the baby looked around and smiled at the face of his mother.

Tip: You diagrammed a participle in sentence # 19. This sentence has a participial phrase. (Page 21 has more information on participial phrases.)

Key	
Rolling onto his stomach, the baby looked around and smiled at the face of his mother.	independent clause
	subject (noun)
the	
	compound verbs (intransitive complete)
and	

around	
at the face	
at	
face	
the	
of his mother	
of	
mother	
his	
Rolling onto his stomach	participial phrase (adjective)
Rolling	participle
onto his stomach	
onto	
	object of the preposition (noun)
his	

SENTENCE # 36

Verbs are words that express action or states of being.

Tip: This sentence has a gerund acting as the object of the preposition *of*.

Key	
Verbs are words	independent clause
	subject (of independent clause) (noun)
	verb (intransitive linking)
	predicate noun
that express action or states of being	
	subject (relative pronoun introducing adjective clause)
	verb (transitive active)
	compound direct objects (nouns)
	coordinating conjunction
of being	
of	
being	

SENTENCE # 37

Butterflies taste food with their feet.

Key	
Butterflies taste food with their feet.	independent clause
Butterflies	
taste	
food	
with their feet	
with	
feet	
their	

SENTENCE # 38

If about 33 million people held hands, they could make a circle around the equator.

Tip: Treat *33 million* as one word.

Key	
they could make a circle around the equator	independent clause
	subject (of independent clause) (pronoun)
	verb phrase
	helping verb
	verb (transitive active)
	direct object (noun)
around the equator	
around	
equator	
the	

	dependent clause (adverb)
If	
	subject (of dependent clause) (noun)
33 million	adjective
about	
	verb (transitive active)
	direct object (noun)

SENTENCE # 39

Dust from Africa can travel across the Atlantic Ocean to Florida.

Key	
Dust from Africa can travel across the Atlantic Ocean to Florida.	independent clause
	subject (noun)
	verb phrase
	helping verb
	main verb (intransitive complete)
from Africa	
from	
Africa	
across the Atlantic Ocean	
across	
Atlantic Ocean	
the	
to Florida	
to	
Florida	

SENTENCE # 40

The most expensive item that ever sold on eBay was a yacht.

Key	
The most expensive item was a yacht	independent clause
	subject (of independent clause) (noun)
The	
expensive	
most	
was	
yacht	
a	
that ever sold on eBay	
that	
sold	
ever	
on eBay	
on	
eBay	

SENTENCE # 41

"The Constitution is the guide which I will never abandon." – George Washington

Tip: Don't diagram *George Washington* since that's not part of the sentence.

Key	
The Constitution is the guide	independent clause
	subject (of independent clause)(proper noun)
The	
is	
	predicate noun
the	
which I will never abandon	
	subject (of dependent clause) (pronoun)
	verb phrase
	helping verb
abandon	
which	direct object (of dependent clause) (relative pronoun)
never	

SENTENCE # 42

Adverbs are words that modify verbs, adjectives, or other adverbs.

Key	
Adverbs are words	independent clause
	subject (of independent clause) (noun)
are	
words	
that modify verbs, adjectives, or other adverbs	
that	subject (of dependent clause) (relative pronoun)
modify	
	compound direct objects
	coordinating conjunction
other	

SENTENCE # 43

A New York man did a continuous series of somersaults for over twelve miles.

Tip: Be careful! You might think *somersaults* is the direct object, but it's not!

Key	
A New York man did a continuous series of somersaults for over 12 miles.	independent clause
man	
A	
	proper adjective
did	
series	
a	
for over twelve miles	
for	
miles	
twelve	
over	
continuous	
of somersaults	
of	
somersaults	

© www.English-Grammar-Revolution.com

SENTENCE # 44

Astronauts orbiting Earth can see 16 sunrises and sunsets in 24 hours.

Tips: Do you remember participles from sentences # 19 and # 35?

16 modifies both direct objects. How can you show that in your diagram? Think about it, and give it a shot!

Key	
Astronauts orbiting Earth can see 16 sunrises and sunsets in 24 hours.	independent clause
	subject
can see	
	helping verb
see	
	compound direct object
16	adjective modifying both direct objects
	coordinating conjunction
orbiting Earth	adjective (participial phrase)
orbiting	participle
Earth	direct object of participle (proper noun)
in 24 hours	
in	
hours	
24	

SENTENCE # 45

People once used breadcrumbs instead of erasers to correct pencil mistakes.

Tips: Sometimes prepositions are made up of more than one word. Treat the words *instead of* as one preposition.

This sentence has an infinitive phrase.

Key	
People once used breadcrumbs instead of erasers to correct pencil mistakes.	independent clause
	subject (noun)
	verb (transitive active)
	direct object (compound noun)
	adverb
instead of erasers	
instead of	
erasers	
	infinitive phrase (adverb)
	infinitive
	direct object of infinitive (noun)
	adjective

SENTENCE # 46

If Earth didn't tilt, we wouldn't have seasons.

Key	
we wouldn't have seasons	independent clause
we	
would have	
would	
	main verb (transitive active)
n't (not)	
seasons	
	dependent clause (adverb)
	subordinating conjunction
Earth	
	verb phrase
did	
	main verb (intransitive complete)
n't (not)	

SENTENCE # 47

A sea turtle can weigh as much as a water buffalo.

Tip: Do you remember elliptical clauses from # 32 and # 34? Remember that some words are implied in elliptical clauses. It's as if this sentence says, "*... as much as a water buffalo (can weigh)*."

Key	
A sea turtle can weigh as much	independent clause
	subject (of independent clause)(noun)
A, sea	
can weigh	
can	
weigh	
much	adverb (modifying "can weigh")
as	adverb (modifying "much")
as a water buffalo (can weigh)	dependent clause (adverb - elliptical clause)
as	adverb (modifying "as")
	subject (of elliptical clause) (noun)
a, water	
	implied verb phrase
	implied helping verb
	implied main verb (intransitive complete)

SENTENCE # 48

Ancient Egyptians believed that a person's soul was located in the heart.

Tip: Do you remember skyhooks from # 31? The word *that* is an expletive that sits on a skyhook.

Key	
Ancient Egyptians believed (that a person's soul was located in the heart)	independent clause (& noun clause acting as direct object of the independent clause)
	subject (proper noun)
believed	
Ancient	
that a person's soul was located in the heart	dependent clause (direct object of "believed") (noun)
that	word introducing dependent clause (expletive) (sits on skyhook)
	subject (noun)
a, person's	
was located	
was	
located	
in the heart	
in	
heart	
the	

SENTENCE # 49

Can you believe that parachutes were invented before airplanes?

Tips: This sentence is a question (interrogative sentence). It's easier to diagram questions if you first turn them into statements. See the key for the statement version of this question.

This sentence has an elliptical clause. *Before* is a subordinating conjunction introducing the elliptical clause *airplanes (were invented)*.

This sentence also has a skyhook! Wow!

Key	
you Can believe that parachutes were invented before airplanes (were invented).	This is how the question looks after we turn it into a statement. Strange!
Can you believe (that parachutes were invented)	independent clause (& noun clause acting as direct object of independent clause)
	subject (of independent clause) (pronoun)

	verb phrase
	helping verb
	main verb (transitive active)
that parachutes were invented	direct object of "can believe" (dependent noun clause)
that	expletive introducing dependent noun clause
	subject (of dependent noun clause) (noun)
were invented	
were	
invented	
before airplanes (were invented)	dependent clause (adverb - elliptical clause)
before	subordinating conjunction
	subject (of elliptical clause) (noun)
	implied verb phrase
	implied helping verb
	implied main verb (transitive passive)

SENTENCE # 50

Conjunctions are words that connect words, phrases, or clauses.

Key	
Conjunctions are words	independent clause
	subject (of independent clause) (noun)
	verb (intransitive linking)
	predicate noun
that connect words, phrases, or clauses	
that	
connect	
words, phrases, clauses	
or	

SENTENCE # 51

Pronouns are words that take the place of nouns.

Key	
Pronouns are words	independent clause
Pronouns	
are	
words	
	dependent clause (adjective)
	subject (relative pronoun introducing dependent adjective clause)
	verb (transitive active)
	direct object (noun)
the	
of nouns	
	preposition
	object of the preposition (noun)

SENTENCE # 52

David, my husband, cooked a lovely dinner, and Marianne, my friend, baked cookies and brownies.

Tip: This sentence has two appositives. You also diagrammed one in # 23.

Key	
David, my husband, cooked a lovely dinner… Marianne, my friend, baked cookies and brownies	compound independent clauses
	coordinating conjunction
David	subject (of first independent clause) (proper noun)
	appositive (noun renaming "David")
my	
cooked	
dinner	
a, lovely	
	subject (of second independent clause) (proper noun)
	appositive (noun renaming "Marianne")
my	
	verb (transitive active)
	compound direct objects (nouns)
and	

SENTENCE # 53

Honeybees can be trained to detect explosives!

Tip: Do you remember that *to + a verb* is an infinitive? This sentence has an infinitive phrase. Infinitives can be nouns, adjectives, or adverbs. What do you think this one is?

Key	
Honeybees can be trained to detect explosives!	independent clause
	subject (noun)
can be trained	
	helping verbs
	main verb (intransitive complete)
to detect explosives	adverb (infinitive phrase) (modifying "can be trained")
	infinitive
explosives	

SENTENCE # 54

Ladybugs squirt a smelly liquid from their knees when they are scared.

Key	
Ladybugs squirt a smelly liquid from their knees	independent clause
Ladybugs	
squirt	
liquid	
a, smelly	
from their knees	
from	
knees	
their	
when they are scared	
when	
they	
are	
scared	

SENTENCE # 55

An electric eel produces a charge that is strong enough to stun a horse.

Key	
An electric eel produces a charge	independent clause
	subject (of independent clause) (noun)
An, electric	
	verb (transitive active)
	direct object (noun)
a	
that is strong enough to stun a horse	
that	
is	
	predicate adjective
enough	
to stun a horse	infinitive phrase (adverb – modifying "enough")
to stun	
horse	
a	

SENTENCE # 56

Marshmallows were originally made from the roots of a plant.

Key	
Marshmallows were originally made from the roots of a plant.	independent clause
	subject (noun)
were made	
	helping verb
	main verb (transitive passive)
	adverb
from the roots	
from	
roots	
the	
of a plant	
of	
plant	
a	

SENTENCE # 57

Hummingbirds are the only birds that can fly backward.

Key	
Hummingbirds are the only birds	independent clause
	subject (of independent clause) (noun)
	verb (intransitive linking)
	predicate noun
the, only	
	dependent clause (adjective)
that	
can fly	
can	
fly	
backward	

SENTENCE # 58

Interjections are words that show emotion.

Key	
Interjections are words	independent clause
	subject (of independent clause) (noun)
	verb (intransitive linking)
words	
	dependent clause (adjective)
	subject (of dependent clause) (relative pronoun)
show	
emotion	

SENTENCE # 59

The face of the Mona Lisa has no eyebrows.

Key	
The face of the Mona Lisa has no eyebrows.	independent clause
face	
The	
has	
eyebrows	
no	adjective
of the Mona Lisa	
of	
Mona Lisa	
the	

SENTENCE # 60

To breathe and swallow at the same time is impossible.

Tip: Remember that *to + a verb* is an infinitive. Infinitives can act as nouns, adjectives, and adverbs.

This infinitive is *to + 2 verbs* acting as a noun (the subject)!

You've never diagrammed a compound infinitive, but use what you know about diagramming infinitives and diagramming compound elements to make an educated guess. ☺

Key	
To breathe and swallow at the same time is impossible.	independent clause
To breathe, swallow	subject (compound infinitive)
and	
is	
impossible	predicate adjective
at the same time	
at	
	object of the preposition (noun)
the, same	

SENTENCE # 61

The kitten constantly meowed because it lost its mother.

Key	
The kitten constantly meowed	independent clause
kitten	
The	
	verb (intransitive complete)
constantly	
because it lost its mother	
because	
it	
lost	
mother	
its	

SENTENCE # 62

People report the most sightings of UFOs when Venus is closest to Earth.

Key	
People report the most sightings of UFOs	independent clause
	subject (of independent clause) (noun)
	verb (transitive active)
sightings	
the, most	
of UFOs	
of	
UFOs	
when Venus is closest to Earth	
when	
Venus	
is	
closest	
to Earth	
to	
Earth	

SENTENCE # 63

Chimpanzees, monkeys, dogs, mice, and guinea pigs have journeyed into space.

Tip: Treat *guinea pigs* as one word. It is a compound noun.

Key	
Chimpanzees, monkeys, dogs, mice, and guinea pigs have journeyed into space.	independent clause
Chimpanzees, monkeys, dogs, mice, guinea pigs	
and	
have journeyed	
have	
journeyed	
into space	
into	
space	

SENTENCE # 64

Did you know that pigs can get a sunburn?

Tip: Turn this question into a statement in order to find the subject more easily.

Do you remember skyhooks from # 31, # 48, and # 49?

Key	
you Did know that pigs can get a sunburn	This is how this question looks after we turn it into a statement.
Did you know (that pigs can get a sunburn)?	independent clause (& noun clause acting as direct object o independent clause)
	subject (of independent clause) (pronoun)
Did know	
Did	
	main verb (transitive active)
that pigs can get a sunburn	
	expletive introducing noun clause (sits on skyhook)
	subject (of dependent noun clause)(noun)
	verb phrase
	helping verb
	main verb (transitive active)
	direct object (compound noun)
a	

© www.English-Grammar-Revolution.com

SENTENCE # 65

The smallest monkey is as tall as a toothbrush.

Tip: This sentence has an elliptical clause.

Key	
The smallest monkey is as tall	independent clause
	subject (of independent clause)(noun)
The, smallest	
is	
tall	
as	adverb
	dependent clause (adverb - elliptical clause)
as	subordinating conjunction
	subject (of elliptical clause) (compound noun)
a	
	implied verb (intransitive linking)
	implied predicate adjective

SENTENCE # 66

Cleopatra became queen of Egypt when she was a teenager.

Key	
Cleopatra became queen of Egypt	independent clause
Cleopatra	
	verb (intransitive linking)
	predicate noun
of Egypt	
of	
Egypt	
	dependent clause (adverb)
when	
she	
was	
teenager	
a	

SENTENCE # 67

Traffic lights were invented before cars.

Key	
Traffic lights were invented	independent clause
	subject (of independent clause) (noun)
Traffic	
	verb phrase
	helping verb
	main verb (transitive passive)
before cars (were invented)	dependent clause (adverb-elliptical clause)
before	subordinating conjunction
cars	subject (of dependent clause (noun)
(were invented)	implied verb phrase
(were)	implied helping verb
(invented)	implied main verb (transitive passive)

SENTENCE # 68

Astronauts' footprints stay on the moon forever because the moon doesn't have any wind.

Key	
Astronauts' footprints stay on the moon forever	independent clause
	subject (of independent clause)(noun)
Astronauts'	
stay	
forever	
on the moon	
on	

moon	
the	
because the moon doesn't have any wind	
because	
moon	subject (of dependent clause) (noun)
the	
	verb phrase
	helping verb
	main verb (transitive active)
n't (not)	
wind	
any	

SENTENCE # 69

"Happy Birthday" was the first song that was transmitted from space to Earth.

Key	
"Happy Birthday" was the first song	independent clause
"Happy Birthday"	subject (of independent clause)(compound noun)
was	
song	
the, first	
	dependent clause (adjective)
that	
was transmitted	
was	
transmitted	
from space	
from	
space	
to Earth	
to	
Earth	

SENTENCE # 70

Clauses are groups of words that have a subject and a verb.

Key	
Clauses are groups of words	independent clause
	subject (of independent clause)(noun)
	verb (intransitive linking)
	predicate noun
of words	
of	
words	
that have a subject and a verb	
that	
have	
subject, verb	
a, a	
and	

SENTENCE # 71

Today, I drank four cups of coffee, and I feel jittery.

Key	
Today, I drank four cups of coffee, I feel jittery	compound independent clauses
and	
I	
drank	
Today	
cups	
four	
	prepositional phrase (adjective)
	preposition
	object of the preposition (noun)
	subject (of second independent clause)(pronoun)
feel	
jittery	

SENTENCE # 72

Independent clauses express complete thoughts.

Key	
Independent clauses express complete thoughts.	independent clause
clauses	
Independent	
express	
thoughts	
complete	

SENTENCE # 73

You have now diagrammed 72 sentences with this program, and you should give yourself a pat on the back.

Tip: *Yourself* is an indirect object.

Key	
You have now diagrammed 72 sentences with this program, you should give yourself a pat on the back	compound independent clauses
	coordinating conjunction
You	
have diagrammed	

© www.English-Grammar-Revolution.com

have	
diagrammed	
now	
with this program	
with	
this	
program	
sentences	
72	
you	subject (of second independent clause) (pronoun)
should give	
should	
give	
yourself	
a	
pat	
on the back	
on	
back	
the	

SENTENCE # 74

If you eat too many carrots, your skin can turn orange.

Tip: Think carefully about the verb *turn*. What kind of verb is it?

Key	
your skin can turn orange	independent clause
	subject (of independent clause) (noun)
your	
can turn	
can	
turn	
orange	
	dependent clause (adverb)
	subordinating conjunction
	subject (of dependent clause)(pronoun)
	verb (transitive active)
	direct object (noun)
many	
too	

SENTENCE # 75

Crocodiles can't stick their tongues out.

Key	
Crocodiles can't stick their tongues out.	independent clause
Crocodiles	
can stick	
	helping verb
	main verb (transitive active)
't (not)	
out	
tongues	
their	

SENTENCE # 76

A coyote can hear a mouse moving under one foot of snow.

Key	
A coyote can hear a mouse moving under one foot of snow.	independent clause
	subject (noun)
A	
	verb phrase
	helping verb
	main verb (transitive active)
	direct object (noun)
a	
moving under one foot of snow	
	adjective (participle)
under one foot	
under	
foot	
one	
of snow	
of	
snow	

SENTENCE # 77

The Leaning Tower of Pisa started tilting before the building was completed!

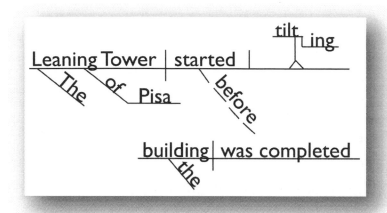

Tip: The proper name of this building is the phrase *Leaning Tower of Pisa.* Even the prepositional phrase is part of its name. Strange!
You can teat *Leaning Tower* as the main subject and *of Pisa* as a prepositional phrase.

Key	
The Leaning Tower of Pisa started tilting	independent clause
Leaning Tower	
The	adjective
of Pisa	prepositional phrase (adjective)
of	preposition
Pisa	object of the preposition (proper noun)
started	
tilting	
before the building was completed	
before	
building	
the	
was completed	
was	
completed	

SENTENCE # 78

Your heart is about the same size as your fist.

Key	
Your heart is about the same size as your fist.	independent clause
	subject (noun)
Your	
	verb (intransitive linking)
about	
	predicate noun
the, same	
as your fist	
as	
fist	
your	

SENTENCE # 79

Dependent clauses don't express complete thoughts.

Key	
Dependent clauses don't express complete thoughts.	independent clause
	subject (noun)
Dependent	
do express	
do	
express	
n't (not)	
thoughts	
complete	

SENTENCE # 80

Prepositional phrases always have a preposition and an object of the preposition, and they always act as adjectives or adverbs.

Key	
Prepositional phrases always have a preposition and an object of the preposition, they always act as adjectives or adverbs	compound independent clauses
	coordinating conjunction
	subject (of first independent clause) (noun)
Prepositional	
have	

always	
preposition, object	
a, an	
and	
of the preposition	
of	
preposition	
the	
	subject (of second independent clause) (pronoun)
	verb (intransitive complete)
always	
as adjectives or adverbs	
as	
adjectives, adverbs	
or	

SENTENCE # 81

Dracorex hogwartsia is a horned dinosaur named after Hogwarts, Harry Potter's school.

Tips: This sentence has an appositive. You diagrammed them in # 23 and # 52.

This sentence also has a participial phrase! (Hint: It starts with *named*.)

Key	
Dracorex hogwartsia is a horned dinosaur named after Hogwarts, Harry Potter's school.	independent clause
Dracorex hogwartsia	
is	
dinosaur	
a, horned	
named after Hogwarts, Harry Potter's school	
named	
after Hogwarts	
after	
Hogwarts	
school	
Harry Potter's	

SENTENCE # 82

Some salamanders can regrow their tails, their legs, and parts of their eyes.

Key	
Some salamanders can regrow their tails, their legs, and parts of their eyes.	independent clause
	subject (noun)
Some	
	verb phrase
	helping verb
	main verb (transitive active)
	compound direct objects (nouns)
	coordinating conjunction
their	
their	
of their eyes	
of	
eyes	
their	

SENTENCE # 83

Koalas and humans have similar fingerprints.

Key	
Koalas and humans have similar fingerprints.	independent clause
Koalas, humans	
and	
have	
fingerprints	
similar	

SENTENCE # 84

Opposite sides of dice add up to seven.

Tip: Treat *add up* as one verb. It's something called a *phrasal verb.* A phrasal verb is a verb plus a preposition or adverb. The words act together to create a meaning different from the original verb.

Key	
Opposite sides of dice add up to seven.	independent clause
	subject (noun)
Opposite	
of dice	
of	
dice	
add up	phrasal verb (intransitive complete)
to seven	
to	
seven	

SENTENCE # 85

African elephants have ears that are shaped like the continent of Africa.

Key	
African elephants have ears	independent clause
	subject (noun)
African	
have	
ears	
that are shaped like the continent of Africa	
	subject (relative pronoun)
	verb (intransitive linking)
	predicate adjective (participle)
	prepositional phrase (adverb, modifying "shaped")
	preposition
	object of the preposition (noun)
the	
	prepositional phrase (adjective)
	preposition
	object of the preposition (proper noun)

SENTENCE # 86

A large python can swallow a whole goat.

Key	
A large python can swallow a whole goat.	independent clause
	subject (noun)
A, large	
	verb phrase
	helping verb
	main verb (transitive active)
goat	
a, whole	

SENTENCE # 87

James loves to go to the movies.

Key	
James loves to go to the movies.	independent clause
	subject (proper noun)
loves	
	infinitive phrase (noun)
	direct object (infinitive) (noun)
	prepositional phrase (adverb) (modifying "to go")
to	
movies	
the	

SENTENCE # 88

Proper nouns name specific people, places, things, or ideas.

Tip: *Specific* is modifying all four direct objects. You diagrammed something like this in #44.

Key	
Proper nouns name specific people, places, things, or ideas.	independent clause
nouns	
Proper	
name	
	compound direct objects (nouns)
or	
	adjective (modifying each direct object)

SENTENCE # 89

Did you know that horses run on their toes?

Key	
you Did know that horses run on their toes	This is the statement version of the question.
Did you know (that horses run on their toes)?	independent clause – interrogative sentence
	subject (pronoun)
	verb phrase
	helping verb
	main verb (transitive active)
	direct object (dependent clause) (noun)
	expletive introducing noun clause (sits on skyhook)
	subject (of dependent clause) (noun)
run	
on their toes	
on	
toes	
their	

© www.English-Grammar-Revolution.com

SENTENCE # 90

A beefalo is a cross between a cow and a buffalo.

Key	
A beefalo is a cross between a cow and a buffalo.	independent clause
	subject (noun)
A	
is	
cross	
a	
between a cow and a buffalo	
between	
cow, buffalo	
a, a	
	coordinating conjunction

SENTENCE # 91 - 95

CURIOSITY QUOTES

Change is good! Let's diagram some quotes!

I've included the names of the people who said these quotes, but don't include those in your diagrams. Have fun!

SENTENCE # 91

"The greatest virtue of man is perhaps curiosity." – Anatole France

Key	
The greatest virtue of man is perhaps curiosity.	independent clause
	subject (noun)
The, greatest	
	prepositional phrase (adjective)
	preposition
	object of the preposition (noun)
is	
perhaps	
curiosity	

SENTENCE # 92

"Intellectual growth should commence at birth and cease only at death."
– Albert Einstein

Key	
Intellectual growth should commence at birth and cease only at death.	independent clause
	subject (noun)
Intellectual	
should commence, cease	verb phrases – compound main verb
and	
	helping verb
commence	main verb (intransitive complete)
at birth	
at	
birth	
cease	main verb (intransitive complete)
only	
at death	
at	
death	

SENTENCE # 93

"Curiosity is one of the permanent and certain characteristics of a vigorous mind." – Samuel Johnson

Key	
Curiosity is one of the permanent and certain characteristics of a vigorous mind.	independent clause
Curiosity	
is	
one	
of the permanent and certain characteristics	
of	
characteristics	
the	
	compound adjectives
	coordinating conjunction
of a vigorous mind	
of	
mind	
a, vigorous	

© www.English-Grammar-Revolution.com

SENTENCE # 94

"When you are curious, you find lots of interesting things to do." – Walt Disney

Key	
you find lots of interesting things to do	independent clause
	subject (pronoun)
	verb (transitive active)
	direct object (noun)
of interesting things to do	
of	
things	
interesting	
to do	
When you are curious	
When	
you	
are	
curious	

SENTENCE # 95

CHALLENGE QUOTE!

"Seize the moment of excited curiosity, for if you let it pass, the desire may never return, and you may remain in ignorance." – William Wirt

Tips: This is the first imperative sentence you've diagrammed in this book. The subject of all imperative sentences is "you understood," and we write it like this: (you).

It (to) pass is an infinitive phrase with a bare infinitive.

Key	
Seize the moment of excited curiosity, the desire may never return, you may remain in ignorance	compound independent clauses (three of them)
Seize the moment of excited curiosity	first independent clause - imperative sentence (command)
(you)	
Seize	
moment	
the	

of excited curiosity	
of	
curiosity	
excited	
for	coordinating conjunction joining independent clauses
the desire may never return	second independent clause
desire	
the	
may return	
may	
return	
never	
if you let it pass	dependent clause (adverb)
if	
you	
let	
it (to) pass	infinitive phrase with bare infinitive (direct object of "let") (noun)
it	
(to) pass	
and	
you may remain in ignorance	third independent clause
you	
may remain	
may	
remain	
in ignorance	
in	
ignorance	

SENTENCE # 96

In Peru, wearing yellow underwear on New Year's Day is considered to be good luck.

Tip: The subject is a gerund phrase, and the direct object is an infinitive phrase!

Key	
In Peru, wearing yellow underwear on New Year's Day is considered to be good luck.	independent clause
	gerund phrase (subject) (noun)
	gerund
	direct object of gerund (noun)

yellow	
	prepositional phrase modifying "wearing"
on	
New Year's Day	
is considered	
is	
considered	
In Peru	
In	
	object of the preposition (proper noun)
	infinitive phrase (direct object) (noun)
	infinitive
	predicate noun (completing the infinitive)
good	

SENTENCE # 97

James felt shy, but he wanted to ask Sara for her number.

Key	
James felt shy, he wanted to ask Sara for her number	compound independent clauses
	coordinating conjunction
	subject (of first independent clause) (proper noun)
felt	
shy	

he	
wanted	
to ask Sara for her number	direct object (infinitive phrase) (noun)
to ask	
Sara	
for her number	
for	
number	
her	

SENTENCE # 98

The largest organ of your body is your skin.

Key	
The largest organ of your body is your skin.	independent clause
organ	
The, largest	
	prepositional phrase (adverb)
	preposition
	object of the preposition (noun)
your	
is	
skin	
your	

SENTENCE # 99

A Harley-Davidson motorcycle was once designed to look like a giant hamburger.

Key	
A Harley-Davidson motorcycle was once designed to look like a giant hamburger.	independent clause
	subject (noun)
A, Harley-Davidson	
was designed	
was	
designed	
once	
to look like a giant hamburger	
to look	
like a giant hamburger	
like	
hamburger	
a, giant	

SENTENCE # 100

A man once rode a bike down the 1,665 stairs of the Eiffel Tower.

Key	
A man once rode a bike down the 1,665 stairs of the Eiffel Tower.	independent clause
	subject (noun)
A	
rode	
once	
down the 1,665 stairs	
down	
stairs	
the, 1,665	
of the Eiffel Tower	
of	
Eiffel Tower	
the	
	direct object (noun)
a	

SENTENCE # 101

The most popular color of car between 2000 and 2005 was silver.

Key	
The most popular color of car between 2000 and 2005 was silver.	independent clause
color	
The, popular	
most	
of car	
of	
car	
was	
between 2000 and 2005	
between	
2000, 2005	
and	
silver	

SENTENCE # 102

Over 100 people in the United States are named Edward Cullen.

Key	
Over 100 people in the United States are named Edward Cullen.	independent clause
	subject (noun)
Over 100	
Over	
100	
in the United States	
in	
United States	
the	
	verb phrase
	helping verb
	main verb (transitive active)
	direct object (proper noun)

SENTENCE # 103

The Spanish flu of 1918, which killed millions of people, originated in Kansas.

Key	
The Spanish flu of 1918 originated in Kansas	independent clause
Spanish Flu	
The	
of 1918	
of	
1918	
	verb (intransitive complete)
in Kansas	
in	
Kansas	
	dependent clause (adjective)
	subject (relative pronoun introducing dependent clause)
	verb (transitive active)
	direct object (noun)
of people	
of	
people	

SENTENCE # 104

The smallest bone in the human body is the stapes, and it is located in the ear.

Key	
The smallest bone in the human body is the stapes, it is located in the ear	compound independent clauses
and	
bone	
The, smallest	
in the human body	
in	
body	
the, human	
is	
stapes	
the	

it	
is located	
is	
located	
in the ear	
in	
ear	
the	

SENTENCE # 105

Reindeer like to eat bananas.

Key	
Reindeer like to eat bananas.	independent clause
Reindeer	
like	
to eat bananas	
to eat	
bananas	

SENTENCE # 106

Dr. Seuss said, "You have brains in your head and feet in your shoes."

Key	
Dr. Seuss said, "You have brains in your head and feet in your shoes."	independent clause
	subject (proper noun)
	verb (transitive active)
You have brains in your head and feet in your shoes	
You	
have	
brains, feet	
	coordinating conjunction
in your head	
in	
head	
your	
in your shoes	
in	
shoes	
your	

SENTENCE # 107

Rattlesnakes are a popular food in some cuisines and are sometimes sold in specialty meat shops.

Key	
Rattlesnakes are a popular food in some cuisines and are sometimes sold in specialty meat shops.	independent clause
	subject (noun)
are, are sold	compound verbs
	coordinating conjunction
are	(the first one)

© www.English-Grammar-Revolution.com

food	
a, popular	
in some cuisines	
in	
cuisines	
some	
are sold	
are	
sold	
sometimes	
in specialty meat shops	
in	
shops	
meat	
specialty	

SENTENCE # 108

The first candy canes were made without stripes.

Key	
The first candy canes were made without stripes.	independent clause
	subject (noun)
	adjectives
were made	
were	
made	
	prepositional phrase (adverb)
	preposition
	object of the preposition (noun)

© www.English-Grammar-Revolution.com

SENTENCE # 109

Australia was once a British prison colony.

Key	
Australia was once a British prison colony.	independent clause
	subject (proper noun)
was	
once	
colony	
	adjectives

SENTENCE # 110

The predictable flooding of the Nile River Valley produced a surplus of crops and fueled the culture of the ancient Egyptians.

Key	
The predictable flooding of the Nile River Valley produced a surplus of crops and fueled the culture of the ancient Egyptians.	independent clause
	gerund phrase (subject) (noun)
	subject (gerund)

The, predictable	
of the Nile River Valley	
of	
Nile River Valley	
the	
	compound verbs (transitive active)
	coordinating conjunction
surplus	
a	
of crops	
of	
crops	
	direct object (noun)
of the ancient Egyptians	
of	
Egyptians	
the, ancient	

SENTENCE # 111

Sinking in the Dead Sea is almost impossible because the water is so salty.

Key	
Sinking in the Dead Sea is almost impossible	independent clause
	gerund phrase (subject) (noun)
	subject (gerund)
in the Dead Sea	
in	
Dead Sea	
the	
is	
impossible	
almost	
	dependent clause (adverb)
	subordinating conjunction
water	
the	
is	
salty	
so	

SENTENCE # 112

A grizzly bear can run as fast as a horse.

Key	
A grizzly bear can run as fast	independent clause
grizzly bear	
A	adjective
can run	
can	
run	
fast	
as	
	dependent clause (adverb - elliptical clause)
as	
	subject (of elliptical clause)(noun)
	adjective
	implied verb phrase
	implied helping verb
	implied main verb (intransitive complete)

SENTENCE # 113

Sharks have eight senses, and humans have only five senses.

Key	
Sharks have eight senses, humans have only five senses	compound independent clauses
	coordinating conjunction
Sharks	
have	
senses	
eight	
humans	
have	
only	
senses	
five	

SENTENCE # 114

Your hair grows faster in warm weather than it grows in cold weather.

Key	
Your hair grows faster in warm weather	independent clause
hair	
Your	
grows	
	adverb
in warm weather	
in	
weather	
warm	
	dependent clause (adverb)
than	
it	
grows	
in cold weather	
in	
weather	
cold	

SENTENCE # 115

All of the blood in your body travels through your heart once per minute.

Key	
All of the blood in your body travels through your heart once per minute.	independent clause
	subject (pronoun)
of the blood	
of	
blood	
the	
in your body	
in	
body	
your	
travels	
through your heart	
through	
heart	
your	
	adverb
per minute	
per	
minute	

SENTENCE # 116

People spend more money on gardening than they spend on any other hobby.

Key	
People spend more money on gardening	independent clause
People	
spend	
money	
more	
on gardening	
on	
	object of the preposition (gerund) (noun)
	dependent clause (adverb)
than	
they	
spend	
on any other hobby	
on	
hobby	
any, other	

SENTENCE # 117

If you add the opposite sides of a die, you will always get seven.

Tip: You've diagrammed this fact before (# 84) but not this exact sentence. Ideas can be written in different ways.

Key	
you will always get seven	independent clause
you	
will get	
will	
get	
seven	
always	
If you add the opposite sides of a die	
If	
you	
add	
sides	
the, opposite	
of a die	
of	
die	
a	

© www.English-Grammar-Revolution.com

SENTENCE # 118

Dolphins sleep with one of their eyes open!

Key	
Dolphins sleep with one of their eyes open.	independent clause
	subject (noun)
	verb (intransitive complete)
	prepositional phrase (adverb)
	preposition
one	
	prepositional phrase (adjective)
	preposition
eyes	
their, open	

SENTENCE # 119

Q is the only letter in the alphabet that does not appear in the name of any of the United States!

Key	
Q is the only letter in the alphabet	independent clause
Q	
is	

letter	
the, only	
in the alphabet	
in	
alphabet	
the	
that does not appear in the name of any of the United States	
that	
does appear	
does	
appear	
not	
in the name	
in	
name	
the	
of any	
of	
any	
of the United States	
of	
United States	
the	

SENTENCE # 120

Did you know that elephants can't jump?

Key	
you Did know that elephants can't jump	This is the statement form of the question.
Did you know that elephants can't jump?	independent clause (interrogative sentence)
	subject (pronoun)
	verb phrase
	helping verb
	main verb (transitive active)
that elephants can't jump	
that	
elephants	
can jump	
can	
jump	
n't (not)	

SENTENCE # 121 - 125

The next five sentences are from <u>Anne of Green Gables</u> by L. M. Montgomery.

SENTENCE # 121

Anne took the dress and looked at it in reverent silence.

Key	
Anne took the dress and looked at it in reverent silence.	independent clause
Anne	
took, looked	
took	
dress	
the	
and	
looked	
at it	
at	
it	
in reverent silence	
in	
silence	
reverent	

SENTENCE # 122

Anne was standing in the new gable room, looking solemnly at three new dresses spread out on the bed.

Tip: *Spread out* is a participle formed from a phrasal verb! You diagrammed another phrasal verb in # 84.

Key	
Anne was standing in the new gable room, looking solemnly at three new dresses spread out on the bed.	independent clause
Anne	
was standing, looking	

was	
standing	
in the new gable room	
in	
room	
the, new, gable	
looking	
solemnly	
at three new dresses	
at	
dresses	
three, new	
spread out on the bed	
spread out	
on the bed	
on	
bed	
the	

SENTENCE # 123

Matthew, who had been hanging about the barn and watching, slipped into the house with the air of a burglar and crept upstairs.

Key	
Matthew slipped into the house with the air of a burglar and crept upstairs	independent clause
	subject (of independent clause) (proper noun)
slipped, crept	
and	
slipped	
into the house	
into	

house	
the	
with the air	
with	
air	
the	
of a burglar	
of	
burglar	
a	
upstairs	
who had been hanging about the barn and watching	dependent clause (adjective)
	subject (of dependent clause)(pronoun)
had been hanging, watching	
had, been	
hanging	
about the barn	
about	
barn	
the	
and	
watching	

SENTENCE # 124

I will try anything and do anything and be anything you want, if you'll only keep me.

Tip: *You want* is a dependent adjective clause modifying *anything*. The word *that* is implied. Diagram it as if the clause is *(that) you want*.

Key	
I will try anything and do anything and be anything	independent clause
	subject (of independent clause) (pronoun)
will try, do, be	
will	
try	
anything	
and	
do	

anything	
and	
be	
anything	
	dependent clause (adjective)
	subject of adjective clause (pronoun)
	verb (transitive active)
	implied relative pronoun introducing adjective clause (direct object)
if you'll only keep me	
	subordinating conjunction
you	
'll keep (will keep)	
'll (will)	
keep	
me	
only	

SENTENCE # 125

Marilla laid her knitting on her lap and leaned back in her chair.

Key	
Marilla laid her knitting on her lap and leaned back in her chair.	independent clause
Marilla	
laid, leaned	
laid	
	direct object (gerund) (noun)
her	
on her lap	
on	
lap	
her	
	coordinating conjunction
leaned	
back	
in her chair	
in	
chair	
her	

SENTENCE # 126

A lizard-like reptile called a tuatara has an eye on the top of its head.

Tips: Treat *lizard-like* as one word.

Called a tuatara is a participial phrase (adjective) modifying *reptile*.

Key	
A lizard-like reptile called a tuatara has an eye on the top of its head.	independent clause
reptile	
A, lizard-like	
	participial phrase (adjective)
	participle
	direct object of participle (noun)
a	
has	
eye	
an	
on the top	
on	
top	
the	
of its head	
of	
head	
its	

SENTENCE # 127

A person who weighs 100 pounds on Earth would weigh 38 pounds on Mars.

Key	
A person would weigh 38 pounds on Mars	independent clause
	dependent clause (adjective)
	subject (of independent clause) (noun)
A	
would weigh	
would	
weigh	
pounds	
38	
on Mars	
on	
	object of the preposition (proper noun)
	relative pronoun introducing adjective clause, subject of adjective clause
weighs	
pounds	
100	
on Earth	
on	
Earth	

SENTENCE # 128

The longest recorded flight of a chicken is 13 seconds.

Key	
The longest recorded flight of a chicken is 13 seconds.	independent clause
	subject (noun)
The, longest	
	adjective (participle)
	prepositional phrase (adjective)
	preposition
	object of the preposition (noun)
a	
is	
seconds	
13	

SENTENCE # 129

Tree wood is a highly organized arrangement of living, dying, and dead cells.

Key	
Tree wood is a highly organized arrangement of living, dying, and dead cells.	independent clause
wood	
Tree	
is	
arrangement	
a, organized	
highly	
of living, dying, and dead cells	
of	
cells	
living, dying	
dead	
and	

SENTENCE # 130

The number of cricket chirps per second can be used to estimate the temperature.

Key	
The number of cricket chirps per second can be used to estimate the temperature.	independent clause
number	
The	
of cricket chirps	
of	
chirps	
cricket	
per second	
per	
second	
can be used	
can, be	
used	
to estimate the temperature	
to estimate	
temperature	
the	

SENTENCE # 131

Oh no, I can't find the shirt that you gave me.

Key	
Oh no, I can't find the shirt	independent clause
	interjection
	subject (of independent clause)(pronoun)
	verb phrase
	helping verb
	main verb (transitive active)
't (not)	
	direct object (noun)
the	
	dependent clause (adjective)
	subject (of dependent clause) (pronoun)
gave	
that	
me	

SENTENCE # 132

A snail would take 220 hours to crawl a mile.

Key	
A snail would take 220 hours to crawl a mile.	independent clause
snail	
A	
would take	
would	
take	
hours	
220	
to crawl a mile	
to crawl	
mile	
a	

SENTENCE # 133

Strawberries have more vitamin C than oranges.

Tips: This sentence has an elliptical clause. It's as if the sentence says:

*Strawberries have more vitamin C than oranges **have vitamin C**.*

Treat *vitamin C* as one noun.

Key	
Strawberries have more vitamin C	independent clause
	subject of independent clause (noun)
	verb (transitive active)
	direct object (compound noun)
more	
	dependent clause (adverb - elliptical clause)
than	
oranges	
(have)	
(vitamin C)	

© www.English-Grammar-Revolution.com

SENTENCE # 134

Your body contains 60,000 miles of blood vessels.

Key	
Your body contains 60,000 miles of blood vessels.	independent clause
body	
Your	
contains	
miles	
60,000	
of blood vessels	
of	
blood vessels	

SENTENCE # 135

Don't judge each day by the harvest that you reap but by the seeds that you plant. - R.L. Stevenson

Tip: This is an imperative sentence.

Key	
Don't judge each day by the harvest but by the seeds	independent clause
	subject (pronoun)
	verb phrase
	helping verb
	main verb (transitive active)
n't (not)	
day	
each	
by the harvest, by the seeds	

© www.English-Grammar-Revolution.com

	coordinating conjunction
by	
harvest	
the	
that you reap	
	subject of adjective clause (pronoun)
	verb (of dependent adjective clause) (transitive active)
that	
by	
seeds	
the	
that you plant	
	subject of adjective clause (pronoun)
	verb (of dependent adjective clause) (transitive active)
	direct object (relative pronoun introducing adjective clause)

SENTENCE # 136

The Milky Way is made of billions of stars.

Key	
The Milky Way is made of billions of stars.	independent clause
	subject (compound proper noun)
The	
is made	
is	
made	
of billions	
of	
billions	
of stars	
of	
stars	

SENTENCE # 137

Rattlesnakes are born without rattles.

Key	
Rattlesnakes are born without rattles.	independent clause
	subject (noun)
	verb phrase
	helping verb
	main verb (intransitive complete)
	prepositional phrase (adverb)
	preposition
	object of the preposition (noun)

SENTENCE # 138

Elephants sometimes make purr-like sounds when they are content.

Key	
Elephants sometimes make purr-like sounds	independent clause
Elephants	
make	
sometimes	
sounds	
purr-like	
when they are content	
when	
they	
are	
content	

SENTENCE # 139

52 of the body's bones are located in the feet.

Key	
52 of the body's bones are located in the feet.	independent clause
	subject
	prepositional phrase (adjective)
	preposition
	object of the preposition (noun)
the, body's	
are located	
are	
located	
	prepositional phrase (adverb)
	preposition
	object of the preposition (noun)
the	

SENTENCE # 140

The skin of a Golden Poison Dart Frog contains enough toxins to kill 100 people.

Key	
The skin of a Golden Poison Dart Frog contains enough toxins to kill 100 people.	independent clause
skin	
The	
of a Golden Poison Dart Frog	
of	
Golden Poison Dart Frog	
a	
contains	
toxins	
enough	
to kill 100 people	
to kill	
people	
100	

SENTENCE # 141

Reaching across the table, John grabbed the shaker of salt.

Key	
Reaching across the table, John grabbed the shaker of salt.	independent clause
John	
Reaching across the table	
Reaching	
across the table	
across	
table	
the	
grabbed	
shaker	
the	
of salt	
of	
salt	

SENTENCE # 142

Most experts believe that birds are descended from dinosaurs.

Key	
Most experts believe (that birds are descended from dinosaurs).	independent clause
experts	
Most	
believe	
that birds are descended from dinosaurs	dependent clause (direct object) (noun)
	expletive introducing noun clause (sits on skyhook)
	subject (of noun clause) (noun)
are descended	
are	
descended	
	prepositional phrase (adverb)
	preposition
	object of the preposition (noun)

SENTENCE # 143

Giant rodents live in the Amazon Rainforest.

Key	
Giant rodents live in the Amazon Rainforest.	independent clause
rodents	
Giant	
live	
in the Amazon Rainforest	
in	
Amazon Rainforest	
the	

SENTENCE # 144

Benjamin Franklin said, "Fatigue is the best pillow."

Key	
Benjamin Franklin said *(Fatigue is the best pillow.)*	independent clause
	subject (compound proper noun)
	verb (transitive active)
	dependent clause (direct object) (noun)
	subject (of noun clause) (noun)
	verb (intransitive linking)
	predicate noun
	adjectives

SENTENCE # 145

Leap and the net will appear.

Tip: Look! It's an imperative sentence.

Key	
Leap, the net will appear	compound independent clauses
and	coordinating conjunction
	subject (of first independent clause) (pronoun)
	verb (of first independent clause) (intransitive complete)
	subject (of second independent clause) (noun)
the	
will appear	
will	
appear	

SENTENCE # 146

Crickets detect sound through their knees.

Key	
Crickets detect sound through their knees.	independent clause
	subject (noun)
	verb (transitive active)
	direct object (noun)
	prepositional phrase (adverb)
	preposition
	object of the preposition (noun)
	adjective

SENTENCE # 147

Ancient Egyptians trained monkeys to dance and play music.

Key	
Ancient Egyptians trained monkeys to dance and play music.	independent clause
Egyptians	
Ancient	
trained	
monkeys	
to dance and play music	
to dance, play	
and	
music	

SENTENCE # 148

A pet goldfish in England lived for 43 years!

Key	
A pet goldfish in England lived for 43 years!	independent clause
goldfish	
A, pet	
	prepositional phrase (adjective)
	preposition
	object of the preposition (proper noun)
	verb (intransitive complete)
	prepositional phrase (adverb)
	preposition
	object of the preposition (noun)
43	

SENTENCE # 149

Blue whales are the largest animals that have ever lived.

Key	
Blue whales are the largest animals	independent clause
Blue whales	
are	
animals	
the, largest	
that have ever lived	
that	
have lived	
have	
lived	
ever	

SENTENCE # 150

The largest dinosaurs were vegetarians.

Key	
The largest dinosaurs were vegetarians.	independent clause
	subject (noun)
	adjectives
	verb (intransitive linking)
	predicate noun

SENTENCE # 151

The smallest frog in the world is the size of a Cheerio.

Key	
The smallest frog in the world is the size of a Cherrio.	independent clause
frog	
The, smallest	
in the world	
in	
world	
the	
is	
size	
the	
of a Cherrio	
of	
Cherrio	
a	

SENTENCE # 152

A highway runs through the middle of a building in Japan.

Key	
A highway runs through the middle of a building in Japan.	independent clause
highway	
A	
runs	
through the middle	
through	
middle	
the	
of a building	
of	
building	
a	
in Japan	
in	
Japan	

SENTENCE # 153

Astronauts have grown potatoes on the space shuttle.

Key	
Astronauts have grown potatoes on the space shuttle.	independent clause
Astronauts	
have grown	
have	
grown	
potatoes	
on the space shuttle	
on	
space shuttle	object of the preposition (compound noun) It's also okay to have "shuttle" as the object of the preposition and "space" as an adjective.
the	

SENTENCE # 154

A comet is a gigantic ball of dirt and ice.

Key	
A comet is a gigantic ball of dirt and ice.	independent clause
comet	
A	
is	
ball	
a, gigantic	
of dirt and ice	
of	
dirt, ice	
and	

SENTENCE # 155

Snowflakes become smaller as the temperature drops.

Key	
Snowflakes become smaller	independent clause
Snowflakes	
become	
smaller	
as the temperature drops	
as	
temperature	
the	
drops	

SENTENCE # 156

One of the largest man-made islands is shaped like a palm tree.

Key	
One of the largest man-made islands is shaped like a palm tree.	independent clause
	subject (pronoun)
	prepositional phrase (adjective)
	preposition
	object of the preposition (noun)
the, largest, man-made	
	verb (intransitive linking)
	predicate adjective (participle)
	prepositional phrase (adverb)
	preposition
	object of the preposition (compound noun) It's also okay to have "tree" as the object of the preposition and "palm" as an adjective.
a	

SENTENCE # 157

A great white shark can weigh as much as 15 gorillas.

Key	
A great white shark can weigh as much	independent clause
	subject (compound noun) It's okay to have "shark" as the subject and "great" and "white" as adjectives.
A	
can weigh	
can	
weigh	
much	
as	
as 15 gorillas (weigh)	
as	
gorillas	
15	
(weigh)	

SENTENCE # 158

Action is the antidote to despair.

This sentence is a quote from Joan Baez.

Key	
Action is the antidote to despair.	independent clause
Action	
is	
antidote	
the	
to despair	
to	
despair	

SENTENCE # 159

The moon does not produce any light of its own.

Key	
The moon does not produce any light of its own.	independent clause
	subject (noun)
The	
	verb phrase
	helping verb
	main verb (transitive active)
not	
	direct object (noun)
any	
	prepositional phrase (adjective)
	preposition
	object of the preposition (noun)
its	

SENTENCE # 160

Did you know that spiders have clear blood?

Key	
you Did know that spiders have clear blood	This is the statement form of this question.
Did you know (that spiders have clear blood)?	independent clause (interrogative sentence)
you	
Did know	
Did	
know	
that spiders have clear blood	
that	
spiders	
have	
blood	
clear	

SENTENCE # 161

A newborn kangaroo is as long as a paperclip.

Key	
A newborn kangaroo is as long	independent clause
	subject (noun)
A, newborn	
	verb (intransitive linking)
long	
as	adverb
as a paperclip (is) (long)	
as	subordinating conjunction
paperclip	
a	
	implied verb (intransitive linking)
	implied predicate adjective

SENTENCE # 162

The average American eats enough hamburger in a lifetime to equal the weight of a car.

Key	
The average American eats enough hamburger in a lifetime to equal the weight of a car.	independent clause
American	
The, average	
eats	
hamburger	
enough	
to equal the weight of a car	
to equal	
weight	
the	
of a car	
of	
car	
a	
in a lifetime	
in	
lifetime	
a	

SENTENCE # 163

Chewing gum burns about eleven calories per hour.

Key	
Chewing gum burns about eleven calories per hour.	independent clause
	subject (gerund phrase)(noun)
	gerund
	direct object of gerund (noun)
	verb (transitive active)
	direct object (noun)
about eleven	
about	
eleven	
per hour	
per	
hour	

SENTENCE # 164

Four-thousand-year-old noodles were discovered in ancient ruins in China.

Key	
Four-thousand-year-old noodles were discovered in ancient ruins in China.	independent clause
noodles	
Four-thousand-year-old	
were discovered	
were	
discovered	
in ancient ruins	
in	
ruins	
ancient	
in China	
in	
China	

SENTENCE # 165

The fastest falcon can outpace a speeding race car.

Key	
The fastest falcon can outpace a speeding race car.	independent clause
	subject (noun)
The, fastest	
	verb phrase
	helping verb
	main verb (transitive active)
race car	
a	
speeding	

SENTENCE # 166

A baking company created a cookie that weighed as much as seven pickup trucks.

Key	
A baking company created a cookie	independent clause
company	
a	
baking	
created	
cookie	
a	
that weighed as much	
that	
weighed	
much	
as	
as seven pickup trucks (weigh)	
as	
pickup trucks	
seven	
(weigh)	i

SENTENCE # 167

A person once hiccuped for 68 years!

Key	
A person once hiccuped for 68 years!	independent clause
	subject (noun)
A	
	verb (intransitive complete)
	adverb
	prepositional phrase (adverb)
	preposition
	object of the preposition (noun)
68	

SENTENCE # 168

Kangaroos do not hop backward.

Key	
Kangaroos do not hop backward.	independent clause
Kangaroos	
do hop	
do	
hop	
not	
backward	

SENTENCE # 169

Some people get goosebumps on their face.

Key	
Some people get goosebumps on their face.	independent clause
people	
Some	
get	
goosebumps	
on their face	
on	
face	
their	

SENTENCE # 170

Food passes through the brains of giant squid on the way to their stomachs.

* Treat *giant squid* as one word. It's a compound noun.

Key	
Food passes through the brains of giant squid on the way to their stomachs.	independent clause
Food	
passes	
through the brains	
through	
brains	
the	
of giant squid	
of	
giant squid	
on the way	
on	
way	
the	
to their stomachs	
to	
stomachs	
their	

SENTENCE # 171

You always see the same side of the moon from Earth.

Key	
You always see the same side of the moon from Earth.	independent clause
	subject (pronoun)
	verb (transitive active)
always	
	direct object (noun)
the, same	
	prepositional phrase (adjective)
	preposition
moon	
the	
	prepositional phrase (adverb)
	preposition
	object of the preposition (proper noun)

SENTENCE # 172

Caterpillars have more muscles than humans.

Key	
Caterpillars have more muscles	independent clause
Caterpillars	
have	
muscles	
more	
than humans (have) (muscles)	
than	
humans	
(have)	
(muscles)	

SENTENCE # 173

A sloth would take a month to travel a single mile.

Key	
A sloth would take a month to travel a single mile.	independent clause
sloth	
A	
would take	
would	
take	
month	
a	
to travel a single mile	
to travel	
mile	
a, single	

SENTENCE # 174

Scuba divers can send postcards from a mailbox that is underwater off the coast of Japan.

Key	
Scuba divers can send postcards from a mailbox off the coast of Japan	independent clause
	subject (compound noun)
	verb phrase
	helping verb
	main verb (transitive active)

© www.English-Grammar-Revolution.com

postcards	
from a mailbox	
from	
mailbox	
a	
off the coast	
off	
coast	
the	
of Japan	
of	
Japan	
that is underwater	
that	
is	
underwater	

SENTENCE # 175

A Slinky can stretch from a sixth-floor window to the ground.

Key	
A Slinky can stretch from a sixth-floor window to the ground.	independent clause
Slinky	
A	
	verb phrase
	helping verb
	main verb (intransitive complete)
from a sixth-floor window	
from	
window	
a, sixth-floor	
to the ground	
to	
ground	
the	

SENTENCE # 176

Pet hamsters can run for miles on hamster wheels.

Key	
Pet hamsters can run for miles on hamster wheels.	independent clause
hamsters	
Pet	
can run	
can	
run	
for miles	
for	
miles	
on hamster wheels	
on	
wheels	
hamster	

SENTENCE # 177

Jellyfish can still sting you when they are dead.

Key	
Jellyfish can still sting you	independent clause
Jellyfish	
can sting	
can	
sting	
	adverb
	direct object (pronoun)
	dependent clause (adverb)
	subordinating conjunction
	subject (of dependent clause) (pronoun)
	verb (intransitive linking)
	predicate adjective

SENTENCE # 178

Bats are the only mammals that fly.

Key	
Bats are the only mammals	independent clause
Bats	
are	
mammals	
the, only	
that fly	
that	
fly	

SENTENCE # 179

The prototype of the original G.I. Joe doll sold for $200,000.

Key	
The prototype of the original G.I. Joe doll sold for $200,000.	independent clause
prototype	
The	
of the original G.I. Joe doll	
of	
doll	
the, original, G.I. Joe	
sold	
for $200,000	
for	
$200,000	

SENTENCE # 180

Sharks can detect a fish's heartbeat before they attack.

Key	
Sharks can detect a fish's heartbeat	independent clause
Sharks	
can detect	
can	
detect	
heartbeat	
a, fish's	
before they attack	
before	
they	
attack	

SENTENCE # 181

Whenever I drive up hills, the car makes a loud noise.

Key	
the car makes a loud noise	independent clause
car	
the	
makes	
noise	
a, loud	
Whenever I drive up hills	
Whenever	
I	
drive	
up hills	
up	
hills	

© www.English-Grammar-Revolution.com

SENTENCE # 182

Catnip can affect lions and tigers.

Tip: Do you know the difference between *affect* and *effect*? *Affect* is usually a verb, and *effect* is usually a noun.

Key	
Catnip can affect lions and tigers.	independent clause
Catnip	
can affect	
can	
affect	
lions, tigers	
and	

SENTENCE # 183

The longest range of mountains is under the sea.

Key	
The longest range of mountains is under the sea.	independent clause
range	
The, longest	
of mountains	
of	
mountains	
is	
under the sea	
under	
sea	
the	

SENTENCE # 184

Is this the way to Grandma's house?

Key	
this Is the way to Grandma's house	This is the statement form of this question.
Is this the way to Grandma's house?	independent clause (interrogative sentence)
	subject (pronoun)
	verb (intransitive linking)
	predicate noun
	adjective
	prepositional phrase (adjective)
	preposition
	object of the preposition (noun)
	adjective

SENTENCE # 185

Prepositions are words that show the relationship between a noun or a pronoun and another element in the rest of the sentence.

Key	
	independent clause
Prepositions	
are	
words	

	dependent clause (adjective)
	subject (of dependent clause) (relative pronoun)
show	
relationship	
the	
between a noun or a pronoun and another element	
between	
	compound objects of the preposition (nouns)
	coordinating conjunction connecting "noun and "pronoun"
	coordinating conjunction connecting "element" and "noun or pronoun"
another	
in the rest	
in	
rest	
the	
of the sentence	
of	
sentence	
the	

SENTENCE # 186

Playing the guitar can be difficult when you are learning.

Key	
Playing the guitar can be difficult	independent clause
Playing the guitar	
Playing	
guitar	
the	
can be	
can	
be	
difficult	
when you are learning	
when	
you	
are learning	
are	
learning	

SENTENCE # 187

Twenty percent of the food that we eat is used to fuel the brain.

Key	
Twenty percent of the food is used to fuel the brain	independent clause
percent	
Twenty	
of the food	
of	
food	
the	
that we eat	
we	
eat	
that	
is used	
is	
used	
to fuel the brain	
to fuel	
brain	
the	

SENTENCE # 188

Running with a friend is a good way to stay fit.

Key	
Running with a friend is a good way to stay fit.	independent clause
Running with a friend	
Running	
with a friend	
with	
friend	
a	
is	
way	
a, good	
to stay fit	
to stay	
fit	

© www.English-Grammar-Revolution.com

TIPS FOR CREATING SENTENCES TO DIAGRAM

If you want to create your own sentence diagrams, follow these tips.

The key is starting with a basic sentence and adding layers.

Here is an example of adding layers to a sentence until it is the appropriate level for you.

1. The dogs howled.

This is short and sweet. It is a nice, simple sentence.

2. The five black dogs howled loudly.

This time, I added some adjectives and an adverb.

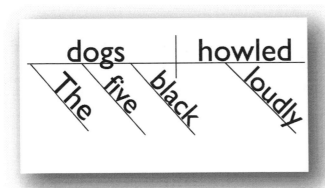

3. Good grief! The five black and white dogs around the corner howled loudly throughout the night.

I added an interjection, a conjunction, and two prepositional phrases.

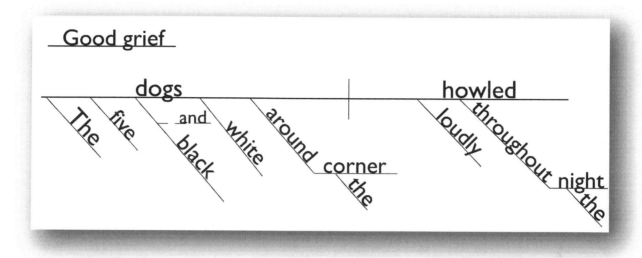

4. Good grief! My neighbor and I hate it when the five black and white dogs around the corner howl loudly throughout the night.

This is a complex sentence. It's made of an independent clause and a dependent clause.

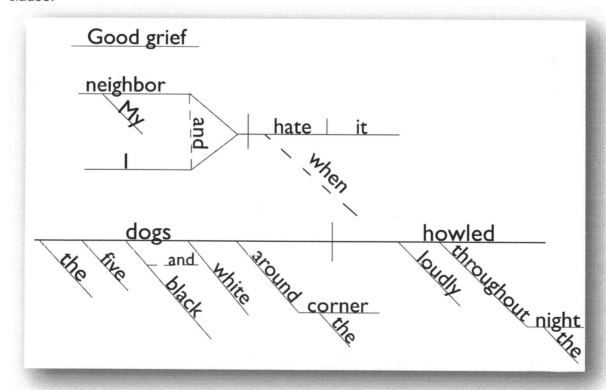

INDEX OF TOPICS

The numbers following the topics below correspond to the sentence numbers. Keep in mind that these numbers are not page numbers.

Dependent Clauses

Dependent Adjective Clauses: 1, 5, 18, 24, 36, 40, 41, 42, 50, 51, 55, 57 58, 69, 70, 85, 103, 119, 123, 124, 127, 135, 149, 174, 178, 185, 187

Dependent Adverb Clauses: 16, 21, 25, 27, 31, 38, 46, 54, 62, 66, 68, 74, 77, 94, 95, 111, 114, 116, 117, 124, 138, 155, 177, 180, 181, 186

Elliptical Clauses (A Type of Adverb Clause): 32, 34, 47, 49, 65, 67, 112, 114, 133, 157, 161, 166, 172

Dependent Noun Clauses: 22, 31, 48, 49, 64, 89, 95, 106, 120, 142, 144, 160

Sky Hooks (In Some Noun Clauses): 31, 48, 49, 64, 89, 120, 142, 160

Verbals

Gerunds: 28*, 36, 62, 77, 96*, 110*, 111*, 116, 125*, 163*

Infinitives: 4*, 27*, 29*, 45*, 53*, 55*, 60*, 87*, 94, 95*, 96*, 99*, 105*, 130*, 132*, 140*, 147*, 162*, 173*, 187*, 188*

Participles: 19, 22, 35*, 44*, 76*, 81*, 85, 122*, 126*, 128, 129, 141*, 156, 165, 166

* = also phrases

Other

Appositives: 23, 52, 81

Imperative Sentences (Commands): 95, 135, 145

Interrogative Sentences (Questions): 49, 64, 89, 120, 160, 184

Phrasal Verbs: 84, 122

CONGRATULATIONS!
YOU JUST DIAGRAMMED 188 SENTENCES!

I hope you had fun. Here are some other super cool sentence diagramming materials.

Get Smart: The Complete Grammar & Sentence Diagramming Solution (Beginner Level)

Do you want to learn grammar the easy way? This program contains in-depth lessons and sentence diagrams that will turn you into a grammar pro. Whether you're a teacher, a student, a writer, an editor, a businessman, a parent, or just a person who loves learning, the easy-to-follow lessons and diagrams will engage you and make you a more confident speaker and writer.

Sentence Diagramming Exercises:
An Introduction To Sentence Diagramming (Beginner Level)

Do you already have some experience with grammar? These step-by-step exercises will teach you how to diagram the eight parts of speech, independent clauses, dependent clauses, verb phrases, prepositional phrases, gerunds, infinitives, participles, and more. This book includes short, simple lessons, and lots of sentence diagramming exercises so that you can learn the basics. When you're done with these exercises, you'll possess a powerful tool for using and understanding language.

Sentence Diagramming Reference Manual: How to Diagram Anything (All Levels)

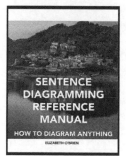

This alphabetized reference manual includes short, simple explanations and easy-to-use sentence diagrams of everything you'll ever want to diagram.

It's the kind of resource you'll reach for when you're learning grammar and when you're a pro who needs a refresher.

Be sure to go to the website and claim your FREE Parts of Speech Quick Guide and grammar newsletter. You'll receive sentence diagramming puzzles and lessons in your inbox every other Tuesday.

www.English-Grammar-Revoultion.com

See you there!

Elizabeth

STAY SMART   WORKBOOK

People with goals succeed because they know

where they are going. It's as simple as that.

~ Earl Nightingale

Made in the USA
San Bernardino, CA
19 March 2016